The Echoes Of Silence

A Poetry Collection

Margo M. Parker

Made with ❤ on the BookLeaf Publishing Platform
www.bookleafpub.in
www.bookleafpub.com

Dedication

To my 9th grade English teacher, Skrbs—
You once told me, "You're going to write something important one day."
As I hold these pages in my hands, I hope I've lived up to that wish.
Thank you for seeing something in me when I couldn't see it in myself.
I only hope this isn't disappointing.

Preface

The Echoes of Silence is not just a collection of poems; it is the voice of a woman navigating the delicate spaces between pain, healing, and understanding. At 30 years old, I have lived through moments that shattered my sense of self and reconstructed me in ways I never imagined. These poems are born from my journey to find meaning in the silence that often surrounds trauma—the kind of silence that speaks louder than words, that can engulf and suffocate, but also teach and transform.

Each poem in this collection represents a step, a breath, or sometimes a silent scream, as I learned to process the complexities of my own pain. Writing became my refuge, a way to translate the unspoken into something tangible, something that could be touched, read, and—most importantly—understood. In these verses, you will find fragments of despair, but you will also find glimmers of hope and resilience. Because trauma, while deeply personal, is something we all share in one form or another, and it is through our collective stories that we find the strength to rise.

I invite you to walk with me through these pages, to listen to the echoes of silence and allow them to resonate with your own experiences. There is power in vulnerability, in the willingness to confront the darkness and allow it to shape us into something greater. This collection is a testament to the healing that happens when we find the courage to speak the things we've kept inside for too long.

Thank you for holding this space with me.

— Margo M. Parker

Acknowledgements

This collection would not have come to life without the support, love, and encouragement of the many people and moments that helped me along the way.

First and foremost, I owe a special thank you to my husband, whose unwavering belief in me carried me through the darkest hours. Your patience, kindness, and understanding have been the foundation upon which this book stands. You are my rock, and this work is as much yours as it is mine.

To my open mic friends, thank you for creating a space where I could share my voice and connect with others who have walked similar paths. Your vulnerability, your strength, and your willingness to listen have been invaluable in shaping the poet I've become.

A heartfelt thanks to JAKL Beer Works, not only for being a place of solace and creativity but for providing the environment where many of these poems were first whispered into existence.

To smooth tequila and strong cups of coffee—your presence has fueled countless nights of writing, reflection, and inspiration. You are the quiet companions of this journey, and I will always be grateful for your steadfast support.

Lastly, to anyone who has ever experienced trauma, found healing, or simply struggled to find their voice—this book is for you. Thank you for walking with me, in silence and in sound, as we all navigate the echoes of our past.

With love and gratitude,

Margo M. Parker

1. Echoes

Empty rooms speak volumes now,
Their silence thick as winter air.
My footsteps bounce from wall to wall,
The only sound that lingers there.

I check my phone — a habit formed
From years of digital embrace.
The screen glows bright, then dims again,
No messages to light this space.

Outside, the world spins madly on,
Through coffee shops and crowded streets.
While here, within these four white walls,
My heart in solitude retreats.

They say alone and lonely are
Two different words, two different states.
But in the quiet of the night,
They blur like shadows through my gates.

I wonder if the stars feel this—
Each one so distant from the rest,
Their light traveling years through space,
To reach another's cosmic breast.

Perhaps there's beauty in this void,
A chance to hear my thoughts ring clear.
But sometimes in the dead of night,
I wish someone else was here.

2. The Echoes of Silence

There are words that live beneath the tongue,
Like creatures in the deepest seas—
Too fragile for the light of day,
Too heavy for the morning breeze.

They gather dust in corner thoughts,
Where memory meets denial's shore.
I've learned to walk around these rooms
Without disturbing what's in store.

Some nights the quiet grows so loud
It pounds against my temple walls.
The things I cannot speak take shape
In shadows dancing down the halls.

My friends ask why I disappear
When certain songs begin to play,
Or why some stories make me fold
Into myself and slip away.

The truth sits patient as a stone,
Worn smooth by years of holding back.
It's funny how a soundless thing
Can leave such thunderous tracks.

I've built a language out of pause,
Of breath caught halfway through the night,
Of sentences that start and stop
Like birds too wounded for full flight.

They say that healing speaks aloud,
That silence is the devil's trade.
But sometimes peace is found between
The words we've lost and those we've saved.

So here I stand in quiet rooms,
Where echoes of the past still ring,
Learning slowly, day by day,
Which parts of silence help me sing.

3. 18

They said your heart was like origami—
delicate folds in all the wrong places.
Three copies where there should be two,
as if your body couldn't help but make
extra room for all the love it held.

The genetic counselor used words like
"incompatible with life"
while I counted your fingers on the ultrasound,
perfect starfish pressed against the screen,
each one a miracle I wouldn't keep.

Ninety-four days.
I memorized your hiccups,
the way you danced at 3 AM,
how you'd settle when I sang—
each moment a photograph I can't frame.

The nurses called you "angel baby"
but that's not what you were—
you were flesh and blood and fighting,
every breath a battle won
until the war became too much.

Sometimes I find myself in baby aisles,
touching tiny socks,
calculating how old you'd be,
what size you'd wear,
which toys you'd love.

They say grief is the price of love
but no one mentions the receipts:
a box of unworn onesies,
a crib that stayed empty,
a number I can't escape.

Eighteen.
Such a small number
to carry such weight—
a chromosome that changed everything,
a love that changed me more.

4. Unlearning Heaven

They taught me to be small—
to fold myself into Eve's shadow,
to wear shame like a second skin.
"Modest is hottest," they said,
while I sweated through summer services,
counting ceiling tiles instead of
the men who watched me anyway.

Sunday school taught me
I was born from a rib,
an afterthought of creation,
made to be helper, never hero.
Funny how they forgot Lilith,
erased every woman who dared
to speak without permission.

Each verse was another cage:
submit, be quiet, cover up.
I learned to cross my legs in church,
to shrink my voice in prayer,
to swallow questions like communion wine
while the pastors' wives smiled vacant smiles,
their hands clasped white in their laps.

God was always "He,"
and somehow He looked exactly like
the men who wrote the rules—
the ones who said my body
was a stumbling block,
my mind a dangerous thing
when filled with anything but scripture.

I tried to be good,
tried to be pure,
tried to be whatever holy meant
in their translation.
But even my salvation
needed a man's approval,
a father's permission,
a husband's guidance.

Now I stand in the ruins
of their paper kingdom,
tear pages from their holy book
to build myself a pyre.
Let them call it rebellion—
I call it resurrection,
rising from the ashes
of their man-made hell.

Their god may have made woman

from a man's spare parts,
but I am remaking myself
from the marble of my rage,
carving out space
in this wide, godless world
where I can finally
stand tall.

The church bells still ring,
but now they sound like warnings,
like the clanging chains
of everything they tried to bind.
I am no longer singing
their gentle hymns of submission—
my throat is full of thunder.
I'm writing my own gospel now.

5. Muscle Memory & Numbers

Yesterday lives in my body—
a tenant that won't leave,
taking up space between
my fourth and fifth rib
where the memories nest.

Check the lock. Again.
Again. Again. Again.
(Four times is safe, they say.
But who are they and why
should I trust them when trust
is what broke me before?)

My shoulders remember things
my mind tries to forget:
the weight of silence,
the crack of sudden sound,
the need to be smaller,
invisible, perfect.

One-two-three-four—
tap the doorframe just so.
The world won't shatter

if I get the rhythm right.
(But it shattered anyway,
didn't it? Even when I
followed all the rules.)

Hypervigilance meets
compulsion in the dark:
both of them screaming
safety's just one more check away,
one more ritual,
one more backward glance.

The therapist says
my brain's just trying
to keep me safe,
but safety feels like
prison feels like
protection feels like
pain.

I count my breaths
while scanning rooms for exits,
measure my steps
while measuring the distance
between trigger and explosion.
Two conditions dancing
in my bloodstream—

a waltz of worry,
a tango of terror.

Sometimes I wonder
which came first:
the need to control
or the knowing that
control is an illusion
wrapped in soap-scented hands
and light switches
flicked eight times clean.

The past lives in my present
like a ghost in the machine,
haunting my habits,
turning routine into religion.
Seven steps to the window,
check the street for dangers,
real and imagined blur
like watercolors in rain.

At night, when the counting stops
and the flashbacks begin,
I hold myself like a child
learning numbers for the first time:
one finger for survival,
two for the breath I'm holding,

three for the years it's taken,
four for the hope I'm keeping,
five for the me I'm becoming—
scarred and scared and
somehow still standing.

The numbers don't save me anymore,
but they keep me company
while I learn to save myself.

6. Hidden Truth

For those of you who don't know
It can make you lose your mind
To remember something clearly
But deny it at the same time
Not 20/20 memories but
I've never said they are
Sometimes flashes of knowledge
Can take your insight far
Because of what I've seen
I'll admit this to be true
I've examined it from all sides
I know I was abused
Truth can be a weapon
Sharper than a sword
Be careful when you're using it
At whom you point it toward
Some accidents may happen
As you find your way
That make you doubt your feelings
Each and every day
I didn't know how to cope
Feeling under attack
Those vivid memories in my head
I begged God -- take them back!

So I denied it happened
And fought the scenes inside
Tried to make them shrink away
In hopes that they would hide
But the truth is static
It does not change its role
Because it is too painful
Or scary for my soul
A long lifetime down the line
I believe it still
And contrary to all attempts
I think I always will

7. Womanhood

I always thought I was born in the wrong time,
A soul misplaced, yearning for a world more kind.
I longed for days when voices could be free,
But then, I looked closer—what did I see?

I dreamt of an age when women stood strong,
Perhaps the Renaissance, where minds did belong—
But I saw the silence, the quiet restraint,
The walls built high, and the rules so quaint.

Was it the 1800s that called my name,
With corsets tight and women to blame?
The suffragists' cry, the gasps for reform,
Yet, they were still shackled by tradition's norm.

The '50s, they seemed to offer some light,
A woman in pearls, in her apron so white—
But behind every smile was a secret so deep,
A quiet revolt, a voice that couldn't speak.

I thought maybe I'd thrive in a world gone by,
Where art and rebellion could reach for the sky.
But then, I realized, as I looked at the past,
That oppression has worn so many masks.

It's not a question of time or place,
But the weight of the world, on a woman's face.
From every era, from every age,
We've fought for freedom, fought to un-cage.

So, perhaps it's not that I was misplaced,
But that every century hides the same race—
To rise, to breathe, to stand and to be,
Not bound by the chains of history's decree.

I wasn't born in the wrong time, you see,
I was born to challenge.
I was born to break free

8. Wishful Thinking

Sometimes I wonder, in quiet despair,
What life would've been like, if she'd been there.
A different mom, a different face,
Would my world have been a softer place?

Dinner dates, with laughter in the air,
Cute gossip shared, and secrets laid bare.
Nail appointments, a salon's sweet hum,
A built-in best friend, where joy would come.

Sipping wine, on the couch we'd sit,
End of a hard day, a moment to quit.
Comfort in her voice, the warmth of her hug,
A bond, unspoken, like a familiar drug.

But that's not the life I have, it's true,
Instead, there's silence, and shades of blue.
Her love is distant, like a star far away,
And I search for her presence, every day.

So sometimes I wonder, and wish for the change,
The mother I longed for, the love that's strange.
But life keeps going, the gaps we must mend,
And I find strength, though it's hard to pretend.

For even without that dream in my mind,
I still keep moving, though lost, undefined.
But deep in my heart, I can't help but see,
What might've been, what could've been for me.

9. Small Talk

I hate small talk with new people
People asking complex questions
Expecting simple answers
Tell me about your family?
Where did you grow up?
I've learned the proper responses
Learning not to dip my toe
Into the pools of stagnant water
So I don't infect you
I formed a mask out of the clay
Sculpted from that toxic lakebed
That I still sometimes wonder
If I ever really truly escaped it
But here I am
Here we are
Dancing in social normalities
Having no idea of the truths I've tortuously become the
keeper of
Then there's those whose interest in the macabre make
them curious
The ones that chose to want me close
Demanding access to my rot
That unprepared you can't dry off
I hate deep talks with new people

asking such complex questions
Not preparing for my answer
Tell me about your family?
Where did you grow up?
I've learned how to be a lifeguard to my own story
Watching for signs of distress
Worried, empathetic, remorseful eyes
Saving them from the stagnant lake
That they thought they could swim in
I don't know how I didn't drown
Waiting for the question that haunts me most
Why?....
Knowing that question has no answer
The emptiness, shame and weight it brings
Watching them see my façade dissolve
Nourishing others pain from those truths
Never getting any comfort of my own
Downplaying the truths I guard and hide
I hate small talk with people
I fear this shame and sadness is the only clean shirt I
have left
The washing machine has been broken for months.
But I'd rather not ruin someone's day with my tragic
honesty
(Where was my protection?)
So instead I'll treat my face like a pumpkin
I'll pretend it's Halloween

I carve it into something acceptable
I laugh and say
"I'm doing alright."
I hate small talk with strangers.

10. 3 minutes and 42 seconds

I heard a song that made me think of you.
The song ended,
And that made me think of you, too.

11. Mother's Medicine

The bottle speaks in amber tones
While I learn to read her silences—
Each evening's ritual of uncorking
Spelled in footsteps up the stairs.

I've memorized the sounds of night:
Ice cubes clinking like wind chimes,
The TV's laugh track covering sobs,
My breathing in the dark.

We play our parts in this dance:
I fold myself smaller, quieter,
A shadow child who knows
Which floorboards won't betray.

Some days she's sugar-sweet,
Promising tomorrow will be different.
Her kisses smell of mouthwash,
Her sorry's taste of gin.

I keep my report cards perfect,
As if good grades might save us both—
Each A a tiny prayer
That she'll remember love.

In school, they teach us
Water makes things grow.
But here, it's mixed with poison
That drowns our family tree.

I've learned to mother my mother,
To clean up morning's evidence,
To tell the neighbors she's just tired,
To believe in somedays.

At nine, I know how to
Pour her into bed,
How to fake her signature,
How to make excuses sing.

They say childhood is magic,
But mine's a vanishing act—
Each day I disappear a little more
Into the girl I have to be.

Sometimes I dream of running,
But guilt has heavier feet
Than any child should carry
Down these whiskey roads.

I store my tears in glass bottles,

Like mother stores her medicine.
One day, perhaps, they'll fill an ocean
Wide enough to sail away.

12. Ordinary Things

I learned to read storms in teacups,
Count seconds between china clinks
And thunderclaps of footsteps—
A meteorologist of rage.

The walls hold breath like smoke
While keys scratch at the door.
I've named all my exits:
Window, stairs, back gate, God.

Love arrives wrapped in apologies,
Beautiful as bruised fruit.
"Just this once," he whispers,
For the forty-seventh time.

I arrange flowers in the vase
He threw last week, each stem
A tiny soldier standing guard
Over our porcelain peace.

My mother asks about the photos,
Why they're face-down like sleeping children.
I tell her about earthquakes, about frames
That slip in summer heat.

The neighbors must know our symphony:
Glass crescendo, door-slam chorus,
My muted aria of please—
But their curtains stay drawn.

I've become an architect of alibis,
Building houses out of cards:
"I fell," "I'm clumsy," "My fault,"
Each lie a brick in my prison.

The shelter lady calls me brave
When brave is just the only
Road left walking. My keys
Jangle like wind chimes of almost.

Tonight, I pack my life in whispers,
Fold memories small as origami,
Leave the ring that once meant forever
On a note that simply says goodbye.

They say leaving is the hardest part,
But they forget about the staying—
Those thousand paper cuts of hope
That bled me nearly dry.

My hands shake like autumn leaves

As I turn the key one final time,
Step into the dark that feels
Brighter than his light ever was.

Freedom tastes like fear at first,
But fear's a door I know how to open—
I've been rehearsing this escape
In dreams for years.

Tomorrow, I'll learn to sleep again
Without mapping exit routes,
To love the sound of silence,
To trust the quiet in my bones.

13. The Archaeology of Smoke

I grew up learning fire safety
from the inside out—
how flames can wear a father's face,
how mothers can burn like matchsticks,
how siblings become smoke signals
in the distance.

No one tells you that after the burning,
you'll spend years excavating ash,
trying to find which parts of you
survived the blaze, which parts
were already ember to begin with.

I thought I was kindling
until I found green shoots
growing through my charred places.
Turns out trauma's a generous gardener,
planting resilience in the ruins.

In therapy, they ask about my childhood home.
I tell them: timber and tinder,
accelerant and aftermath.
They note how I still check

every room for exits,
how I flinch at the strike
of a match.

Some nights I dream in infrared,
my memories all heat signatures
and thermal readings.
Which parts burned hottest?
Which parts stayed cool enough
to shelter something soft?

I'm learning that identity
is what remains after the fire—
not just scar tissue and survival skills,
but the quiet spaces between burns,
the parts that refused to ignite.

Yesterday, I held a candle
without trembling.
Named its light beautiful
instead of dangerous.
Called its warmth friend
instead of enemy.

Sometimes I catch my reflection
and see smoke for skin,
ember for eyes.

But underneath this ash-gray dawn,
I'm finding bones of steel,
a heart of unexploded things,
a spine made from all the ladders
I built to climb myself to safety.

They say you can't step
in the same fire twice.
But no one mentions how long
you'll carry its light,
how you'll learn to read
by its glow, how you'll find
yourself written in the language
of what wouldn't burn.

I'm excavating myself
from the family bonfire,
discovering that I'm not
what they tried to incinerate—
I'm what rose
from their attempt.

Now I understand:
some things need burning
to become themselves.
Like pine cones releasing seeds,
like forests after wildfire,

like me—
finally learning
that I'm not the house
that burned,
but the phoenix
they failed to notice
nesting in the attic.

14. Nocturne's Promise

The light makes promises in gold—
productivity and proper paths,
straight lines drawn on calendar days,
achievements hung like medals
on the breast of morning.

But darkness,
darkness asks for nothing,
spreads its ink-stained fingers
across my restless mind
and whispers: dream.

Light demands witness,
counts my hours like currency,
measures worth in visible things—
in crossed-off lists
and mirror-perfect smiles.

While night wraps me
in possibilities unnamed,
lets me shed my daily skin
and wear instead
the constellations of my wanting.

Dawn brings her brass band
of should and must,
her marching orders
sealed with sunrise,
her gleaming expectations.

But here, in shadow's grace,
I paint futures with closed eyes,
build castles from the stuff
of maybe, write stories
in the margins of midnight.

Light shows the world
its own reflection,
every flaw in sharp relief,
every dream reduced
to practical dimensions.

Dark holds space
for what we dare not speak,
cradles wild imaginings
like secrets in its palm,
asks only that we trust its depth.

Morning will come
with its golden guarantees,
its promises of purpose,

its well-lit paths
to someone else's truth.

But night knows
the sweetness of uncertainty,
how freedom tastes
when no one watches,
how dreams grow best in shade.

So let the light make
all its bright demands—
I'll keep my alliance
with the dark,
where possibilities breathe wild and deep,

Where I can be
both lost and found,
where every shadow
holds a door
to worlds unnamed and waiting.

For in this soft obscurity,
I finally understand:
light may promise progress,
but darkness promises
nothing but myself.

15. The Art of Being Broken

I used to think broken meant ruined—
like china shattered on kitchen floors,
like mirrors cracked to seven years' bad luck,
like things that couldn't hold their purpose anymore.

But here's what I've learned about breaking:
each fracture line maps a journey,
each crack catches light differently,
each piece holds a story of touching.

There's Amanda in my laugh now,
the way it breaks high and wild—
a gift from summer nights when we rode
with windows down and stars for company.

Michael left his silence in my hands,
taught me how to hold grief
like a bird with broken wings,
how to heal through holding still.

Shana's courage lines my spine,
a brass-bright fragment from the day
she showed me how to stand
when the world said kneel.

Even those who hurt me
left their glitter in my wounds—
teaching me how pain, when transformed,
becomes wisdom's constellation.

I'm held together by spider silk
and midnight conversations,
by borrowed strength
and inherited resilience.

My grandmother's hymns
hum in my broken places,
and my first love's goodbye
taught my heart to bend, not end.

Some days I'm a mosaic
of everyone I've ever loved,
their colors catching light
at different angles.

Other days I'm stained glass,
my breaks transformed
into something holy,
something that needs breaking
to be beautiful.

I've stopped trying to hide
the places where I'm pieced together.
Each seam tells a story
of survival and connection.

Now when I meet someone new,
I listen for the music
of their particular breaking,
the way their pieces sing.

We're all walking galleries
of everyone we've met—
masterpieces of mosaic,
proof that broken things
know how to hold light best.

So let me break a little more,
make room for new voices,
new colors, new ways of being
put back together.

Because I'm learning that wholeness
isn't about being unbroken—
it's about having enough cracks
to let everyone's light in.

And these fragments I've become?

They're not wreckage but windows,
not wounds but weathering,
not endings but openings
through which love learns
new ways to enter.

16. Eighteen

At eighteen, my mind was spring flowers—
fresh buds of possibility,
until his fists became the frost
that withered everything green.

Between bottle-throws and baby cries,
my synapses started misfiring,
like Christmas lights with broken bulbs,
dim, then dark, then sparking wrong.

The child's eyes watched everything—
two moons reflecting my galaxy
of bruises, while my thoughts turned
to static, white noise, survival mode.

They say the brain is plastic,
malleable as modeling clay,
but mine hardened too early,
set in patterns of flinch and flee.

Now I catch myself sometimes,
searching for the girl I was
before fear became my native tongue,
before I learned to speak in whispers.

Time has softened some edges,
but certain circuits stay scrambled—
like a record scratched too deep
to ever play the same song twice.

Yet here I am, still breathing,
still teaching my rewired mind
how to trust the gentle things:
dawn light, soft voices, open doors.

17. Love Songs for the Aftermath

You said you loved me
in the language of bruised wrists
and borrowed blame—
called it passion when your fingers
left continents of purple
across my atlas skin.

Remember how I learned to speak
in weather patterns?
"I fell" became my forecast,
"I'm clumsy" my daily high,
"It was my fault" the chance
of storms, always storms.

They don't tell you how love
can sound like keys in a door,
how your heart can learn
to beat in tempo with footsteps,
how you can taste fear
in the back of your throat
and still call it romance.

You wore devotion like brass knuckles,

each "I love you" a closed fist
against my ribcage—
and still I stayed,
believing love was supposed to hurt,
that passion meant blood under fingernails
and apologies like morning coffee:
bitter, routine, necessary.

Now I count the ways
my body remembers you:
in flinches and phantom pains,
in the way I still check
all the locks twice,
in how I apologize
for taking up space,
for breathing too loud,
for existing at all.

They say the body keeps score—
mine plays your greatest hits
on repeat:
that time you said I was beautiful
while wrapping your hands around my throat,
how you kissed the bruises better
before making new ones,
how you loved me most
when I was disappearing.

I'm learning now that love
shouldn't taste like copper,
shouldn't sound like breaking glass,
shouldn't feel like holding your breath
until the danger passes.

But some nights I still dream
in the color of your anger,
wake up reaching
for the pieces of myself
I left behind
in your bedroom,
in your fists,
in your version of love.

18. Growing Pains

At twenty-seven, my friends live in rectangles—
little boxes on my phone where we trade
heart emojis and "we should catch up soon"s,
while calendar squares fill with overtime
and doctor's appointments no one reminds us to make.

Remember when friendship meant
sitting cross-legged on bedroom floors,
sharing secrets like communion wafers,
time stretching endless as summer?
Now we measure it in coffee dates
scheduled three weeks in advance,
canceled twice, rescheduled once.

My mother never warned me how adulthood
tastes like takeout eaten alone,
how silence becomes a roommate
that never pays rent but always stays,
how Friday nights transform
from possibilities into permissions
to rest, finally rest.

The group chat goes quiet for weeks.
Someone got married. Someone had a baby.

Someone moved across the country.
We double-tap their highlights,
type "miss you!" under filtered photos,
while distance grows between us
like ivy on old brick walls.

There's a specific sadness
to watching your people become memories,
to realizing no one knows
when you changed your coffee order
or started taking evening walks
or learned to sleep on the other side of the bed.
The small evolutions happen alone.

They don't tell you how growing up
means growing apart,
how birthday parties become birthday texts,
how "best friends forever"
turns into "friends who used to be"
while you're too busy paying bills
to notice the transition.

Yet sometimes, at 2 AM,
when the world feels too big
and my apartment too empty,
I scroll through old photos
and remember how it felt

to be known completely,
to exist in the plural—
we, us, ours—
before life taught us
the fine art
of becoming singular.

19. Unlearning the Sharp Edges

I used to think self-care was another job
I was failing at—
another box left unchecked,
another way to prove
I couldn't get it right.

Drink more water (you're dehydrated again)
Exercise daily (why are you so lazy?)
Meditate (your mind's too messy)
Journal (you missed three days)
Face masks (your skin's a mess)
Yoga (you're not flexible enough)
Green smoothies (you're never healthy enough)
Eight hours sleep (you're always tired)
Deep breathing (you can't even relax right)

Until one morning,
watching steam rise from my coffee,
I didn't check my phone,
didn't count the calories,
didn't time how long I sat there.
Just watched the sun paint
gold squares on my kitchen floor

and felt, for a moment,
like a person who deserves
small, uncounted joys.

Maybe self-care isn't military precision.
Maybe it's not measuring worth
in steps or ounces or minutes.
Maybe it's letting yourself eat breakfast
at 3 PM because that's when you're hungry.
Maybe it's napping without setting an alarm.
Maybe it's leaving dishes in the sink
because your body is begging for rest.

What if we treated ourselves
like something tender and new—
a just-unfurled leaf,
a first attempt,
a morning glory opening
not because it must,
but because the sun
feels nice on its petals?

What if self-care meant
putting down the measuring tape,
the stopwatch,
the endless lists of improvements?
What if it meant saying:

Here I am,
imperfect and unfinished,
worthy of gentle things.

I'm learning that some days,
self-care is brushing my teeth,
and some days it's dancing in the kitchen,
and some days it's crying in the car,
and all of these are valid ways
to carry myself through the world.

The softest revelation:
I don't have to earn my existence.
Don't have to optimize every breath.
Don't have to turn kindness
into another kind of violence.

I can just be here,
breathing unscheduled air,
taking up space,
letting my edges stay soft,
learning to hold myself
like something precious
and breakable
and already
enough.

20. The Language of Different Stars

Nobody tells you how lonely
the waiting rooms will become—
fluorescent lights humming
above endless clipboards,
each one asking you to quantify
your child in numbers
that never add up right.

Other mothers talk about milestones
like stepping stones across a pond,
while we're here building
our own constellations,
celebrating the first word
at age four,
the first step at two,
the first friend at eight—
each one a supernova
in our private galaxy.

I've learned to speak
in acronyms and diagnoses,
to fight insurance companies
with the fury of a prophet,

to translate my child's silence
into ninety-minute evaluations
while strangers nod
and scribble notes.

The grocery store is a battlefield—
every flickering light,
every sudden noise,
every well-meaning stranger
who doesn't understand
why my nine-year-old
still melts down in aisle three.
I've gotten good at carrying
both my child and our dignity
out to the car,
where I sometimes cry
behind sunglasses
before driving home.

There are nights I lie awake,
calculating therapies like bills,
wondering if I'm doing enough,
if I should push harder,
do more, be more,
while my child sleeps
wrapped in their weighted blanket,
perfectly themselves,

untroubled by my doubts.

My friends post about
soccer games and dance recitals.
We celebrate when my child
learns to zip their coat,
to look in someone's eyes,
to tell me their heart hurts
without using fists.
These victories don't fit
in Facebook status updates.

I've become fluent in
a different kind of motherhood—
one that measures progress
in inches, not miles,
that knows the weight of words
like "never" and "might not,"
that understands love
sometimes looks like
four hours of occupational therapy
and remortgaging the house
to pay for summer programs.

They say God only gives you
what you can handle.
I want to tell them

God should have checked with me first,
because some days
I'm held together
with coffee and duct tape,
running on fumes and fear
and fierce, desperate hope.

But then there are moments—
when small hands find my face
in the dark,
when a new word appears
like a gift,
when laughter bubbles up
unexpected and pure—
and I realize
I'm not just carrying this child
through the world.
This child is teaching me
how to see it differently:
not broken, just speaking
in languages I'm still learning,
showing me courage
I didn't know I had,
loving me with a heart
that knows no conditions.

It's the hardest thing I've ever done,

this daily dance of too much
and not enough,
of pride and pain,
of letting go of the child
I thought I'd have
to embrace the one
who's teaching me
that different isn't less—
it's just a map
to a world
I never knew
I needed
to find.

21. Small Mercies

It's in the coffee mug appearing
beside your laptop before dawn,
steam rising like a whispered
good morning.

In the way the cat's bowl
is filled without discussion,
and someone remembers to buy
the bread you prefer.

Love moves in quiet currencies:
a jacket draped over sleeping shoulders,
the last cookie left untouched,
knowing it's your favorite.

It's there in folded laundry,
still warm from the dryer,
in the gas tank filled without
being asked, in saved crossword
puzzles from Sunday papers.

In the gentle acceptance of your
off-key singing, in the shoulder
that bears your worst days,

in the hands that know
when to hold and when
to let you pace the floor
at midnight.

These are the atoms of caring:
small, invisible until you learn
to look closely at the ordinary,
to find infinity in dishes dried,

in borrowed umbrellas returned,
in doors held open just a moment longer,
in all the ways we say I love you
without saying anything at all.